Amaryllis, Paperwhit

MW01132856

Growing, Propagating and Reblooming Your Holiday Plants

by Miranda Hopkins

First Published in 2012 by Cardigan River LLC
Copyright © 2012 Miranda Hopkins
Photo credits: Cover: iStockPhoto.com
All other photos: Fotolia.com

ISBN 10: 098844335X
ISBN 13: 978-0-9884433-5-8

Disclaimer

No part of this publication may be reproduced or transmitted in any form or by any means, mechanical or electronic, including photocopying or recording, or by any information storage and retrieval system, or transmitted by email without permission in writing from the publisher.

While all attempts have been made to verify the information provided in this publication, neither the author nor the publisher assumes any responsibility for errors, omissions, or contrary interpretations of the subject matter herein.

This book is for educational purposes only. The publisher and authors of this instructional book are not responsible in any manner whatsoever for any adverse effects arising directly or indirectly as a result of the information provided in this book. The views expressed are those of the author alone, and should not be taken as expert instruction or commands. The use of any information provided in this book is solely at your own risk.

Adherence to all applicable laws and regulations, including international, federal, state and local governing professional licensing, business practices, advertising, and all other aspects of doing business in the US, Canada or any other jurisdiction is the sole responsibility of the purchaser or reader.

Any perceived slight of any individual or organization is purely unintentional.

Table of Contents

Introduction

Once winter hits and bare trees and bushes remove all vestiges of the growing season, many families opt to bring a bit of the outdoors inside. One fun and very easy way to do that is by adding live plants to the holiday decorating scheme. The bright red, white or coral color of poinsettia flowers always reminds people that the winter holiday season is here. You can force bulbs indoors so that your house bursts with the white flowers of Paperwhite Narcissus bulbs, or the many varieties of color combinations of different amaryllis species. If you are looking for a gift for someone who is hard to shop for, or a token gift to give to a host or hostess when you attend a holiday party, maybe these winter holiday plants will fill that bill.

Disclaimer

Around the end of the year, you're likely to hear stories about the toxicity of poinsettia plants. The plants themselves are not toxic, according to MedicineNet (http://www.medicinenet.com/script/main/art.asp?articlekey=55606). The site provides further information from POISONINDEX, the information source that is used by national poison control centers, which suggests that a 50 pound child would have to ingest 500 leaves of a poinsettia plant before they showed any signs of toxicity. The confusion may be due to the fact that poinsettia belongs to the genus Euphorbia, and that genus does have some have some very toxic plants.

Chapter 1: Amaryllis

Hippeastrum "Double Record" © Svetlana Nikolaeva – Fotolia.com

History and Background

Amaryllis is one of two common names for the genus Hippeastrum, which is also the proper botanical name for all of the plants that are recognized as "Amaryllis." The other name by which it is commonly known is Barbados Lily. The name Hippeastrum comes from the Greek word for "horse star." That is a reference to the plant's large, star-shaped flowers. Early classical Greek writers also used the word as a woman's name, and it is found in some classical Greek pastoral poems.

The true Amaryllis, A. *belladonna*, is a native of South Africa. The plant and some of its relatives were discovered sometime during the early 18th century in South America. A few Amaryllis species were originally natives of Africa, however, most originated in the tropical Americas, mainly South America.

The other South American Hippeastrum are spread out across Argentina, Brazil, Paraguay, Peru and Uruguay. A. *belladonna,* is characterized by wide, trumpet-shaped blossoms. In its native habitat, the plant blooms from late fall into early winter.

At the time of its discovery, Amaryllis was used as both the common and scientific name. There are roughly 75 species in the Hippeastrum genus, all of which are known as Amaryllis. Additionally, Amaryllis belongs to the large Amaryllidaceae family, and all members of this family are related to daffodils. There are many complex and technical botanical differences that distinguish different species, but aside from the botanical differences, the main way in which hippeastrums differ is in their place or region or origin.

Earliest Appearance in Europe

In the late 17th century, a small number of species were brought to Europe. These plants were different than the species seen today. They all lacked the broad, trumpet-shape that is the hallmark of today's amaryllis plants. Nonetheless, their flamboyant flowers convinced plant breeders of their promise.

Early Efforts in Developing New Varieties

Amaryllis breeding history spans more than 200 years. Most cultivars on the market today are Dutch. By the middle of the 1700's, scientists were trying to create hybrid plants by using different species. The result of this cross breeding is plants with large flowers in pink, red and white, and many different combinations of these colors. Hybrids have come from parent plants such as Hippeastrum *leopoldii,* H. *aulicum*, H. *elegans*, H. *puniceum*, H. *solandriflorum*, H. *striatum*, and H. *puniceum*.

Earliest Hybrid

In 1799, a British watchmaker created the first hybrid when he crossbred H. *reginae*, (a plant that featured five-inch bright red flowers,) with H. *vittatum*, (a plant that had six-inch long flowers with red-and-white stripes.)

Earliest Introduction to the United States

The fact that bulbs could easily withstand the cross-Atlantic trip undoubtedly meant that they came to the US soon after their introduction to the British. They weren't commercially available, however, until the 1930's. Up until the 1950's, they were primarily only seen in the south. There, they were used as an addition to flower beds. Amaryllis bulbs provided color in the Southern garden when no other bulbs were in bloom. No one recognized the potential to use amaryllis bulbs as indoor houseplants prior to the 1950's.

Developing Hybrids in Florida

Orlando, Florida breeders Henry Nehrling and Theodore Mead developed hybrids in the early 20th century. Most of the commercially available hybrids today contain DNA from some of the main Hippeastrum species, including:

- *H. vittatum* Herbert

- *H. leopoldii* Dombrain

- *H. reginae* Herbert

- *H. pardinum* (Hook.f.) Lemaire

- *H. puniceum* (Lamarck) Kuntze

- *H. aulicum* Herbert

Hybridization between inter-specific species was eventually focused on tetraploid hybrids, that is, plants with three sets of chromosomes. There are four real reasons for using tetraploid hybrids, and those include:

1. The existing presence of certain desirable characteristics, including the size of flowers, the number of scapes, and most importantly, stabilized plant health.

2. Crossing diploid species, those with two sets of chromosomes, with tetraploid hybrids creates sterile offspring.

3. Using tetraploid hybrids is often necessary because diploid varieties aren't available.

4. Since many diploid species and diploid hybrids are self-incompatible, that problem can be avoided by using tetraploid hybrids.

New Breeding Trends

As the Hippeastrum market leaders, the Dutch know that they need to bring a fresh look to their old standards. To do that, and to find new hybrids they must look to both amateur and professional breeders. Most of the newer Dutch hybrid cultivars are triploid species. Another new trend is seen in the dwarf hybrid species that Japan is introducing. Some of the newer Japanese hybrids include multiflora species (those that produce many buds,) "blue" flowers and "spider" varieties.

Amaryllis Breeding at the University of Florida

The University of Florida breeding program started in 1987. The primary goal of University of Florida breeders was to produce unique flower color combinations and shapes. They also wanted to create plants that produce flowers with more buds and more fragrant flowers. Another important goal was to create more disease resistant plant varieties.

The secondary goal was to produce cultivars that are more well suited to use in the landscape, that have high quality foliage, and that are capable of producing the greatest number of offsets. The offsets are necessary for propagation.

Commercial Hybrid Propagation

Hybrid plants are produced from seed. The process of propagating commercial Amaryllis, – those that are sold to wholesalers and retail distributors, are cloned. The cloning is done by removing small offset bulbs that grow off the parent plant, a natural process that occurs with all bulbs, rhizomes and tubers. The small bulbs are then grown into larger bulbs. The process is constantly self–perpetuating as small offset bulbs are removed from the new plants and so on. Anyone who grows Amaryllis can do this themselves, provided they have the necessary growing conditions and patience to see the process through.

Popular Amaryllis Varieties

Single–Blooming Varieties

- 'Apple Blossom' – a variety that is characterized by soft pink–and–white flowers.

- 'Green Goddess' has nearly all white flowers, with the exception of a green throat.

- 'Minerva' is a readily available and very popular variety that is characterized by nearly all red flowers except for the white star that forms near the flower's throat.

- 'Picotee' is a white flower that has tinges of red at the edge of each flower petal.

- 'Red Lion' is a deep, almost crimson red variety.

- 'Prince Carnival' is a lesser known variety that has basically white flowers that are streaked with red stripes on the flower petals.

- 'Exotic Star' has flowers that have a cream to greenish-colored background that is covered with raspberry-colored stripes in a brushstroke-like pattern.

- 'Red Velvet' is a variety whose large bulbs can measure between 30 and 32 centimeters in circumference. The large bulb produces two or three stems, and each stem will hold anywhere from four to six flowers. The flowers are the color of red velvet.

Amaryllis similar to Picotee © Harald Biebel - Fotolia.com

Double-Blooming Varieties

- 'Double Picotee' has the same coloration patterns as single 'Picotee,' but it differs in that the stems produce two flowers at one time rather than one.

- 'Lady Jane' has flowers that are rose-pink in color, and each petal has a white vertical streak that runs down the center of the petal.

- 'Pasadena' is characterized by solid red flowers with white streaks on the petals.

Miniature Varieties

Miniature varieties are those whose stems are shorter than the 18 to 36 inch range that is normal for other varieties.

- 'Baby Star' has bright red flowers with a white star at the flower center near the throat.

- 'Fairytale' is a pure white flower that has raspberry stripes.

- 'Pink Star' is a variety that has pink-rose colored petals and a white star that forms at the center of the flower.

White Flower Farm (http://www.whiteflowerfarm.com) is one of the best suppliers and one that has a huge number of different varieties, including some of the South African varieties. The Amaryllis Bulb Company (http://www.amaryllis.com/) is another good source with a wide selection from which to choose.

General Care Requirements

Indoor Care Requirements

Plant bulbs in a loose, well-drained soil medium. Allow the top ¼ inch of the bulb to protrude above the soil. After planting, make sure that bulb is firmly anchored so the plant doesn't topple over once the stems start to get tall. You can use special bulb stakes that will provide the necessary stabilization to hold the stem upright, and clay pots also offer security. After planting, place the bulb in a location where the temperature remains consistent between 55 and 60 degrees F. These cool temperatures will assure you of healthy spikes, and by continuing to provide this and consistent light, and regular watering in small amounts, your bulb will produce two, or even three additional spikes from which flowers will emerge.

An amaryllis bulb with three spikes © Dmitry Ejov – Fotolia.com

Allow your bulb to continue growing after blooming, but once all of the flowers die and the spike is not sending up more shoots or producing more flowers, cut the flower stalk off near the top of the bulb. Don't worry if there is liquid that runs out of the cut flower stalks; it is a sign that the plant has received plenty of water. Cutting the stems off allows your bulb to store up nutrients that will sustain it during dormancy and provide the nutrition it needs to put forth the first new growth when you force it again.

Outdoor Care Requirements

Amaryllis are suited to growth outdoors in USDA hardiness zones 9 and 10. You may be successful at growing them and getting them to re-bloom in USDA hardiness zones 7 and, provided you cover the bulbs and ground surrounding them with a heavy layer of mulch – at least, this was based on the information provided in the North Carolina State

University Amaryllis Fact Sheet. This will ensure that soil temperatures below the surface remain more consistent. Loosen the soil and plant the bulb where the base is 8 inches below the surface. You can plant in groupings of three for a nice cluster look. Otherwise plant one to two bulbs together and allow a distance of between six and 12 inches between bulbs. They are suitable as border plants or bedding plants. As long as the bulbs are in the active growing phase, keep the soil moist, but not overly wet. Excess moisture can cause bulbs to rot. Plant stems typically grow to 24 to 36 inches tall.

Problems and Diseases

Amaryllis are hardy bulbs that don't often contract diseases or suffer from pest invasions, but since it is a possibility, it is worth mentioning different diseases and pest problems. By understanding what makes the bulbs more susceptible to problems, you will be prepared to deal with any situation that might arise.

Diseases that affect the Amaryllis include Red Scorch (Staganospora curtisii,) and Cerscospora leaf spot, both of which are serious fungal diseases. Fungal diseases are often caused by too much moisture. Be sure to plant bulbs in clean, sterile soil. Water plants close to the soil to avoid splashing water on the leaves, and allow plants to dry out before watering again. When forcing bulbs, you want to keep the soil moist, but not wet. To deal with these diseases, you can spray them with a broad-spectrum fungicide. An organic, all natural product that works well as fungicide is NEEM oil. It is available at many large garden centers under a variety of brand names.

Types of Bulb Rot and Viruses

Fusarium is one type of bulb rot. It is a bacteria that affects many types of plants. Plants that suffer from bacterial bulb rot cannot be treated. The bulbs must be destroyed. Do not put diseased bulbs into your compost heap because the bacteria can contaminate the entire heap. Hippeastrum mosaic virus is similar to the type of mosaic virus that affects tomato plants. It is also untreatable. Bulbs that sit in excessively moist soil, or that aren't cleaned and dried properly for storage during dormancy are more prone to contracting severe enough diseases that the bulb can't be salvaged.

Pest Problems

Pest problems are more prevalent in plants that are grown outdoors in the field for commercial propagation and sales, or those that are grown in greenhouses and shade houses. For those grown in greenhouses or shade houses, the most common pest problems are mealybugs, scales and thrips. Pest problems that are more common in the field include caterpillars, lubber grasshoppers, and occasionally, snails and slugs. In Florida and Louisiana, there is a yet-to-be identified weevil that causes problems for plants. The pest entered the United States via Louisiana and spread to Florida from there.

Getting Bulbs to Bloom Again

Many people who grow Amaryllis bulbs over the holidays don't save their bulbs or allow them to continue to grow after they bloom. As with other bulbs, Amaryllis are meant to bloom repeatedly. Getting a bulb to bloom again is very simple. Once the bulb flowers, cut off the flower stalks and allow the leaves to continue to grow. Continued growth will allow the bulb to develop a stronger root system and store up more nutrients to keep the plant alive during dormancy.

The bulb should go into dormancy for eight to nine weeks starting around September 1st. If you are growing your plant indoors, cut back any leaves. You can also remove the bulb from the soil, clean it off and allow it to dry thoroughly. Then place it in a cool dark place where temperatures range from 45 to 50 degrees. Allow it to remain there until the beginning of the second week of November. Then replant the bulb and care for it as you have in the past. This should ensure that your bulb produces flowers right around Christmas time, and it should continue to flower until well after the New Year.

Propagation Methods

Most propagation methods require that plants grow for a minimum of two years before they are well enough established to use for any type of propagation. Tissue culture and twin scale cuttage require that bulbs grow for two years before they are ready to use. Plants do not typically produce seeds for a minimum of three years. The easiest, most straightforward and full-proof method of propagation is twin scale cuttage.

Twin Scale Cuttage

Twin scale cuttage is only done on bulbs that have grown for at least two years. Using a sterile knife, slice the bulb lengthwise into equal-sized sections. Make sure that each division has an attached portion of the basal plate and two concentric bulb scales. You don't have to plant each division in individual pots until a bulblet forms. Use a rich, sterile growing medium that drains well.

Plant deep enough to cover the basal plate completely. The basal plate is the bottom core-like portion of the bulbs where the roots emerge. Once planted, place the cut sections in a warm but shady location.

Keep the growing medium moist but not wet. If the soil is too wet, the new plants are at risk for contracting fungal disease or developing bulb rot, and the disease can spread throughout the soil. Allow each section to continue growing until they develop a couple of leaves. At that time, you can transplant them into smaller individual pots.

Chapter 2: Paperwhite Narcissus Bulbs

Paperwhites growing outside © Zina Seletskaya – Fotolia.com

Background History and Origins

The genus Narcissus belongs to the Amaryllis family. The Amaryllidaceae family includes roughly 15 different bulb species, and they are either herbaceous or perennial. Both paperwhite narcissus and the familiar yellow daffodils are types of Narcissus. The botanical classification for paperwhites is *Narcissus tazetta ssp. papyraceus*. The Latin meaning for the botanical name couldn't be more appropriate in its description of the flowers. The translation is roughly "the lily with small papery cups."

The scientific name for Paperwhite Narcissus is Narcissus *tazetta.* Narcissus comes from the Greek word "Narke," the same word from which narcotic (the term used for certain types of medicines,) is derived. Pliny believed that the Narcissus flower was capable of producing a stupor in people. The ancient Greeks believed that the fragrance of narcissus flowers could cause headaches, provoke madness in people, or at the worst, kill them.

According to Greek mythology, Narcissus developed a near obsession with his own reflection. The Greek Gods responded to this by turning him into a lily – as punishment. The mere mention of this might lead people to believe that there is some relationship between the origin of the flower's name and the story, but that isn't believed to be the case.

The word "tazetta" has origins as an old southern European name. The Italian word "tazza" means cup, and so the addition of the word "tazetta" as the Narcissus cultivar known as Paperwhite is no doubt, related to the cup shape found on the crown of Paperwhite Narcissus flowers.

Narcissus flowers have clearly existed for over 2500 years, as is evident from Homer's description of it in a "Hymn to Deter."

> *"The Narcissus, wondrously glittering, a noble sight for all, whether immortal Gods, or mortal men; from whose root an hundred heads spring forth, and at the fragrant odour thereof all, the broad heaven above and all the earth laughed, and the salt-wave of the sea."*

Relationship to Daffodil

The Mediterranean Narcissus is closely related to the popular outdoor early spring daffodil. One big difference between the daffodil and the narcissus is the fact that narcissus cannot withstand freezing temperatures, so it can't be planted in the ground or overwintered in USDA hardiness zones where there are sub-freezing temperatures. Places such as southern California, Arizona and Florida are ideally suited to outdoor winter growth of paperwhites. Although paperwhites should be hardy to zone 8b, if you want to grow them outside, cover the ground around the bulbs with a heavy insulating layer of mulch to protect them from possible freezing temperatures.

Storing Bulbs Prior to Planting

If you purchase your bulbs in early fall and plant them right away, you won't get blooms for over a month. If, however, you purchase the bulbs in early fall and hold off on planting them until February, you may be able to get your bulbs to bloom in as few as two weeks. The bottom line is that the longer you store your bulbs, the faster you'll get flowers when forcing them indoors. For this reason, you might want to consider next year's paperwhite bulbs the previous year. That way, when you give them to someone as a holiday gift the following year, the recipient will be thrilled by how quickly the bulbs produce flowers.

Forcing Bulbs Indoors

Paperwhite Narcissus bulbs are ideal for indoor growth. They generally take anywhere from five to eight weeks from planting to produce flowers, so expect to see your flowers sooner than you would with an Amaryllis bulb. Because paperwhites are harvested from their native growing habitat in the Mediterranean areas, (most come from Israel,) they don't have to undergo chilling prior to planting.

What is Meant by the Term "Forcing Bulbs?"

Forcing bulbs is a process whereby bulbs that are grown under artificially created conditions, can bloom at a desired time. It is a process that is frequently used for both amaryllis and paperwhite narcissus bulbs to "force" them to flower around the winter holidays. Some bulbs require a cooling period in which they are subjected to temperatures of between 35 and 50 degrees F in preparation for growth and subsequent blooming. Paperwhites don't need this.

How to Force Paperwhite Narcissus Bulbs

The two main ways to force paperwhites are either by planting them in a well-draining growing medium or by placing the bulbs in a container which consistently keeps the entire body of the bulb above and out of water. Both methods are equally effective; it is a matter of personal preference, or a question of whether you want to use the paperwhites and their container as part of your winter holiday decorating scheme.

Growing Paperwhites Without Soil

Supplies for Water Forcing Paperwhite Narcissus:

- A container that has no drainage holes – including shallow glass or ceramic dishes, bulb pans, any type of decorative household dish or bowl. It should be no less than two-to-three inches deep.

- River stones, gravel, pebbles, marbles, beach glass or clear glass beads that are used in floral arrangements. Most of these things are easily found in garden centers or craft supply stores.

- Paperwhite narcissus bulbs – large firm bulbs are the best.

How to Arrange Paperwhites in Water:

1. Fill your container with stones or pebbles, leaving at least an inch of space between the top of the stones and the rim of the dish. Your container and stems need to provide support for your bulbs to keep them from flopping over when stems grow long enough so that the bulbs are top-heavy.

2. Fill the container with enough water so that the water line lies just below the top of the rocks.

3. Place the bulbs on top of the stones. You want to place as many bulbs in the dish as possible. This will reduce the amount of big empty spaces you have between bulbs once the stems emerge and the bulbs finally flower.

4. After placing the bulbs in the container and securing them in the gravel or stones, pile more stones around each individual bulb so that the upper 2/3 of the bulb sticks out above the stones.

*IMPORTANT CONSIDERATION –

Don't allow the bulbs to touch water directly. They will get plenty of water from transpiration and evaporation. Once the roots emerge, they'll grow more rapidly and start touching the water, so that will provide more direct access to water. Bulbs that sit directly on the water may develop mold and rot. Check on the bulbs every day to make sure that the water level is consistent. If your home is very dry, you may need to replenish the water supply every day.

Until the bulbs develop a substantial root system and the first shoot or shoots emerge, keep the bulbs in a cool, dark or dimly lit place. A basement or semi-heated garage is perfect. You want to try to mimic the natural conditions they grow in outdoors after they are planted in the fall.

Check on the bulbs every one-to-two weeks to see how root development is progressing. When you check on the bulbs, give each one a gentle tug to see if there is root growth. You will be able to tell because the bulb won't move as easily. As soon as you can tell that the bulb has a well-established root system and the first shoots have emerged, you can bring the bulbs out into the light. Place them in a location where they will get bright, but indirect light.

Depending on the temperatures within your house, they should bloom within two to three weeks after you bring them out into the light. Maintain cool temperatures in your house at all times. The ideal temperature range is between 60 and 65 degrees F. If that is not possible, try to maintain a daytime temperature of no higher than 70 degrees F, and nighttime temperatures in the low 60 degree F range. If your house gets too warm, your bulbs will grow too quickly and the stems will become leggy and flop over.

One Way to Get Paperwhite Stems to Stand Upright

To ensure that the bulbs stand upright, you can purchase special stakes or plant rings. You can create your own attractive support system by using green bamboo stakes that are available at garden centers, super stores and home improvement stores. Instead of using ordinary string or twine, tie natural or holiday colored raffia around the stakes, creating a natural net through which the stems can grow.

Other Decorative Touches

Instead of using ordinary gravel, consider using brightly colored marbles or clear or colored stones that are used for securing flowers in vases. Even colored gravel for fish tanks will work well. Instead of using ordinary bulb pans, purchase inexpensive decorative holiday dishes, colored glass bowls or other ceramic containers. Just be sure that any dish you use doesn't have any holes in it.

Using Alcohol to Get Paperwhites to Stand Upright

Also called pickling, or "ginning up paperwhites," the theory behind using alcohol to keep the stems of paperwhite narcissus bulbs standing upright is that the alcohol reduces the growth of paperwhite stems. William B. Miller, a professor of horticulture and the Director of the Flower Bulb Research Program at Cornell University in Ithaca,

New York is credited with finding this innovative solution for the bothersome problem that plagues narcissus growers. Narcissus bulb stems have a tendency to grow very tall, and as a result, they get floppy and fall over entirely. Dr. Miller and his fellow researchers discovered what is now referred to as the Cornell "secret."

Their research found that by using a highly diluted amount of alcohol, they were able to reduce the length of paperwhite stems by anywhere from one-third to ½ the usual height to which the stems grow. They also discovered that their process didn't compromise either flower production or bloom time at all.

How to Make an Alcohol Solution to Inhibit Paperwhite Stem Growth

Start your paperwhites according to the steps above. Before you do this, make sure you have some distilled spirits or liquor on hand. Do not use wine or beer because of their high sugar content. You can use anything such as gin, tequila, rum, vodka or whiskey. Once the bulbs have produced roots and the first shoots appear, pour all of the water out of the growing dish. Create your solution by mixing one part alcohol to 7 parts of water. That means you need to add seven times more water than the amount of liquor you use. By doing this, you will have reduced the alcohol content of the solution to five percent.

You will want to mix up enough of the solution so that you can replenish it as you would have done with water, as the bulbs absorb it or some evaporates. You will use the alcohol solution in place of water the entire time you're forcing the bulbs. This will stunt the growth of stems, but it won't compromise the extent of flower production or bloom time. Because your stems are reduced in length, you won't have to worry about providing any supports to keep them from flopping over.

Substitutions

If you don't have distilled spirits or other hard liquor on hand, you can substitute rubbing alcohol or isopropyl alcohol. It contains a significantly higher alcohol content, so you will need to dilute your solution even more, should you use isopropyl alcohol. Use one part alcohol and dilute that with ten or even eleven parts of water. Avoid using any type of alcohol that has a high sugar content.

Although the researchers at Cornell haven't yet determined exactly why growth is stunted, for now, they are speculating that the cause may be a phenomenon known as "water stress" In simple terms, the addition of alcohol to the water makes it harder for the bulbs to absorb as much water as they would without it. Without the water, the bulb isn't getting as much food, and the stems can't grow as quickly. That doesn't explain why the alcohol has no impact on flower longevity or production.

*A Word of Caution

Humans aren't immune to alcohol poisoning or toxicity and plants aren't either. If you use too much alcohol, the bulbs may suffer from alcohol toxicity.

Not Suited to Re-Forcing Again

Paperwhite Narcissus that are forced indoors are very difficult to re-force into bloom again. Professional growers like Joe Garafalo of the University of Florida Miami-Dade County Cooperative Extension, who grow paperwhites en mass for sale to the nursery and flower retail industry, advise people against trying to re-force the bulbs again. His own experience has taught him that the quality of blooms after re-forcing are so disappointing that the results aren't worth the effort.

Growing Paperwhite Narcissus Bulbs Outdoors

According to Joe Garafalo, paperwhites are suited to outdoor growth from zones 7b and above. He suggests that they can tolerate outdoor growth in zones that get no colder than about +10 degrees F.

In proper outdoor conditions, paperwhites will re-bloom, but not without baking in the hot summer sun so that they can "ripen" properly. This makes places like south Florida or other places in U.S.D.A. Hardiness zones 9-10 ideal locations in which to grow paperwhites outdoors.

Bulbs begin to send shoots up in the fall. Flowers usually emerge either before the leaves or at the same time as the leaves. After flowering, the bulb will continue to grow as it stores up a supply of food to keep it nourished throughout dormancy and as the bulb prepares to begin a new growth cycle.

Ideal Outdoor Growing Conditions

The ideal climate in which to grow paperwhites outside is one in which the winters are typically cool and wet and the summers are hot. The amount of rainfall the bulb receives during the summer months is not as important as the rainfall it receives during the fall and winter months when it is actively growing.

Paperwhites are adaptable in many environments, including places along riverbanks, along the sea coast, in meadows, throughout rocky areas, or in woodland area. The most important requirements for success with paperwhites is a place where there is full sun, loose well-draining soil, and adequate water.

Chapter 3: Poinsettias

Pink Poinsettias © Margo Harrison – Fotolia.com

History and Origin of Poinsettias

Always familiar in retail stores everywhere during the holidays, poinsettias are as much a part of Christmas tradition as are Amaryllis and Paperwhites. It is the #1 selling flowering plant in the United States, as sales for these attractive plants exceed 70 million plants each year. The plant is widely used to decorate homes, offices and other businesses during the winter holidays.

U.S. Ambassador to Mexico Joel Robert Poinsett

Poinsettia plants get their name from Joel Robert Poinsett, since he brought the plants into the United States, and subsequently introduced the country to them in 1825. He was the first U.S. Ambassador to Mexico. Although he attended medical school and trained to be a doctor, Poinsett's great passion was botany. He was able to nurture that passion in the greenhouses he had on his Greenville, South Carolina plantations.

The story of Poinsett's introduction to the plants that bear his name tells of a visit he made to the Taxco area of Mexico. While there, he discovered a plant that had unique, bright red flowers. He liked the plants so well that he sent some of them back to South Carolina so he could propagate them. His successful efforts allowed him to share plants with friends and botanical gardens. Not surprisingly, the plant was ultimately named after him. The botanical name for poinsettia is *Euphorbia pulcherrima*, which translates as "the most beautiful Euphorbia." A German taxonomist gave the plant its botanical name in 1833.

The Story of Pepita and the Discovery of the Poinsettia

There is another story that is supposed to explain the plant's origin. The story is about a poor Mexican girl whose name was Pepita. Pepita was walking to the chapel with her cousin to attend the Christmas Eve service. Unable to afford a gift to offer to the Baby Jesus at the chapel nativity scene, Pepita was embarrassed. Her cousin tried to assure her that the love she felt was far more important than any material gift. She stopped along the side of the road and gathered some wild weeds and created a bouquet out of them.

After entering the chapel with her cousin, she walked up the aisle to the alter, remembering what her cousin had told her – that "even the most humble gift, given in love will be acceptable in his eyes." Those words bolstered her confidence and she left the bouquet at the alter. She walked away, and then, as if by a miracle, those weeds were turned into beautiful red flowers. All of the congregants in the chapel and Pepita and her cousin were sure that they'd just witnessed a miracle. From that point on, those red flowers were known as "Flowers of the Holy Night," or "Flores de Noche Buena." Those very flowers are known today as the poinsettia plant.

Poinsettia Structure and How to Choose Your Plants

The colorful part of the poinsettia plant is not the flower. It is known as the bract. The center part of the plant, which is called the cyathia, is the actual flower. When looking for plants to purchase, look for but brightly colored bracts. You want plants that have very few flowers that have already produced pollen. Plants should have vibrant bracts and little to know pollen production. If bracts aren't bright and if pollen is present on the flowers, the plants are past their peak of freshness. Examine the foliage on plants. Although the darkness of leaf color varies from variety to variety, you should see a lot of lush leaves. The absence of foliage is another indication that the plant isn't fresh and healthy.

Bract Color

Look for bracts that are covered in color. Bracts vary in color from traditional red to marbled, peach-colored, pink, speckled, white, or yellow. The bract is the part of the plant with the vivid color, so the richness and vibrancy of the color are crucial. Avoid buying plants that have green at bract edges. Look for plants that have lots of dark green leaves. You want the foliage to extend down the entire length of the stem.

Plant Shape and Proportion

The height and proportion of the plant is partly dependent on the size of the pot. The circumference and height of the plant should be proportional to the size of the pot. Healthy plants should be aesthetically appealing. The standard for a plant that has good proportions is that the plant should be roughly 2 ½ times taller than the diameter of the pot it is growing in.

Avoid purchasing plants that are packed in decorative mesh, paper or plastic sleeves. These things prevent the plant from getting adequate air circulation, and it limits growth space. Not only does it hasten the deterioration of the plant's health; it can also conceal the very things that you want to avoid.

How to Care for Poinsettia Plants

Poinsettias need bright, but indirect light for a minimum of six hours a day. You can protect them from direct light with either a filtering blind or sheer curtains or drapes. Protect plants from excessive heat, cold, ventilation, vents or anything that may cause dryness. Daytime temperatures should be consistent at no more than 70 degrees F.

During the active growing phase and just prior to blooming, keep plant soil moist, but not wet. To determine if the plant needs water, stick your finger in the soil. If the uppermost layer of soil is dry, then water the plant. Be sure to saturate the soil when watering, but don't allow the plant to sit in water. Too much water can cause root rot.

Unless you live in a very temperate climate, grow your plants as houseplants. They aren't well suited to outdoor growth because of their extreme sensitivity to cold, freezing temperatures and rain. In places where winter temperatures outside don't drop below 55 degrees F, and where daytime temperatures are mild, plants can be placed outside in protected places such as enclosed porches.

After Holiday Poinsettia Care

Regrettably, many people do not keep their poinsettia plants after the holiday season. Plants continue to look good through March, and with proper care after the seasonal color display, plants can produce attractive flowers and bright-colored bracts year after year.

Continued care should include regular watering when the soil is dry and exposure to indirect light. Once the weather warms so that the nighttime temperature doesn't drop below 55 degrees F, place plants outside. By March or April, bracts lose their attractive color. Cut plant stems back so they are no more than about 8 inches tall. Continue to care for plants as before, and new growth will appear by May.

While plants are in active growth period during spring, summer and fall, water regularly and fertilize your plants with an all-purpose fertilizer every two-to-three weeks. Transplant your plants into pots that are no more than four inches larger than the original pot they were growing in. The ideal growing medium should contain a lot of organic matter in addition to clean soil. Peat moss or leaf mold are good sources of organic matter. Throughout summer and up to September 1, prune your plants to maintain their shape.

Getting Plants to Rebloom

Poinsettias are considered short-day plants because they develop buds and ultimately flower at the time of the year when nights are longer, which is during fall. Although different cultivars flower at different times, most varieties are in full-bloom between

November and December. To be assured of Christmas blooming, expose your plants to at lease six, but no more than eight hours of bright sun or light from October 1st to early December.

Because plants need 14 hours of complete darkness during the time leading up to their blooming, you will need to move them to a place that is completely dark or cover each plant with a box for the hours of required darkness. Maintain nighttime temperatures between 60-and-70 degrees F and continue your regular regime of fertilizer and water throughout the pre-blooming time period.

New, Different and Novelty Varieties and Cultivars

Poinsettia varieties and cultivars get their names from a variety of sources. The trend towards naming them for holiday-inspired foods began in 2000. It produced some unusual cultivar names such as Christmas Cookie, Santa Claus Candy (a cultivar that has light pink bracts that are covered with red highlights,) Peppermint, Champagne, and Plum Pudding. The reason for naming cultivars for foods stemmed from a desire to use names that had never been used.

The development of new varieties corresponds to consumer demand. There are also cultivars that are bred to be new additions to existing series. These varieties are given distinguishing names so as to avoid any confusion over the names of the original cultivars. Most poinsettias that are sold are red, a fitting choice because red is a traditional Christmas color. As consumer interest in pink, white and mixed shades and varieties increases, so does the demand for plants with unusual color combinations, bract shape, form and size.

Growers also showcase their new varieties by changing the look of bracts or leaves. One of the 21st century additions to the list of available varieties is one that has leaves that resemble oak leaves, complete with the distinctive oak leaf points. Holly Point is a variety that retains the desired Christmas feeling, but with a very unusual twist. The cultivar is characterized by bright red bracts and yellow and green variegated leaves.

Some of the more popular cultivars include:

- Candy Cane – a plant that has white bracts with red speckles.

- Carousel – a variety with twisted red bracts.

- Christmas Feelings – a cultivar with cream and pink fringe.

- Cinnamon Star – a variety that has a mixture of cream and pinkish-peach bracts.

- Cranberry Punch – a cultivar whose bracts are a mixture of bright red and pink.

- Lemon Drop – a variety that is characterized by pale yellow bracts.

- Plum Pudding – a cultivar that is characterized by plum colored or dark purplish-red bracts.

Novelty Cultivars

- Holly Point – a cultivar that is supposed to be reminiscent of Christmas holly with its red bracts and contrasting variegated foliage.

- Jingle Bells – a variety that is characterized by red bracts that are dotted with pink spots.

- Mars Pink – cultivar that is characterized by a combination of dark and light pink bracts.

- Marble – a variety that has white bracts that are covered with marbled areas of pink.

- Monet – a cultivar that is a combination of cream, rose-colored pink, and pink bracts.

- Winter Rose – a unique variety whose bracts are crinkled so that they form the shape of a rose. It is available in various colors.

New Cultivars for 2012

- For 2012, the North American Poinsettia Trials focused on 21 new varieties. Although all 21 new varieties may not appear in breeder catalogs, suppliers may be able to get some of the cultivars that aren't listed. Customer demand has pushed growers to produce more red varieties, and that trend continues. Some new non-red varieties are introduced as part of a series, while some are introduced to improve on older varieties. In addition, two of the new cultivars for 2012 are novelties. The new introductions for 2012 include:

New Red Cultivars for 2012

- 'Bella Italia Red' – a variety that looks like a red ball.

- 'Charon Red' – a cultivar that is characterized by flat bright-red medium-sized bracts and dark green leaves.

- 'Dramatic Red' – a variety that has long, large bright-red bracts that are bold enough to make a statement.

- 'Early Mars Red' – a cultivar that flowers in mid-November and that is a companion to the 'Mars Red' cultivar that was introduced in 2009. 'Early Mars Red' is taller than 'Mars Red.' and although the bracts on both varieties are the same color, 'Early Mars Red' has dark green leaves.

- 'Matinee' – is a variety that is characterized by distinctive long, pointed red bracts that form a starbust-like effect.

- 'Overture' – a cultivar that is characterized by large, round, bright-red bracts.

- 'Pandora' a variety whose dark red bracts flower in mid-season. Although it is supposed to be a compact variety, breeders didn't see that in the trials.

- 'Portia Red' is a cultivar whose small bracts are a medium-reddish color. Young plants have upright bracts, but that doesn't last as the plant ages.

- 'Premier Red' is a variety with medium to large-sized bright red bracts. The bracts on this compact variety show their color in early November – unlike many other varieties.

- 'Talitha Red' is a cultivar that produces medium-red-colored bracts that create the distinctive classic ball for which poinsettias are known. Bract edges had a slight curl and as plants age, bracts hang down.

- 'Tikal Red' a variety that is similar to 'Advent Red,' it is characterized by large, medium-red colored bracts.

- 'Titan' – a variety that is true to its name in strength, but it isn't excessively vigorous.

New White Cultivars for 2012

- 'Candlelight White' – is a variety that was designed to coordinate with 'Christmas Day Red.' Both grew to nearly the same height and develop their bract color and flower blooms in mid season, or within a couple of days of one another. Medium-sized bracts are creamy white and have some visible green veining. It is suited to multiple container sizes and will look great if planted together with 'Christmas Day Red.'

- 'Saturnus White' is a cultivar that belongs to the 'Saturnus' series. It is characterized by small, creamy-white bracts with contrasting dark-green foliage. It reaches its peak of attractiveness at mid-season, around the same time as other 'Saturnus' cultivars in the series. It is a more compact variety than the other members of the series.

New Pink Cultivars for 2012

- 'Christmas Beauty Pink' – a cultivar that belongs to the 'Christmas' series flowers in mid-season, but slightly later than other members of the series. The medium-sized bracts begin as dark pink when plants are young, changing to medium-pink, and ultimately to salmon with age.

- 'Jubilee Pink' – a variety that flowers at about the same mid-season time as 'Jubilee Red.' It is characterized by medium-sized bracts that are dark pink when young. Bract veins are even darker pink. Bracts lighten with age, following the pattern of most pink cultivars, including the gray cast that older bracts on pink plants develop.

- 'Saturnus Pink' – is a cultivar that is characterized by small bracts with dark pink veins and an overall bract color that is medium pink. Unlike other pink cultivars whose leaves have a gray-green cast, 'Saturnus Pink' has brighter green leaves. Bracts and flowers are at their peak a few days later than 'Saturnus Red.'

2012 Novelty Cultivars

- 'Early Monet' is an updated, more compact version of the older 'Monet' cultivar. This particular cultivar is one of the most important novelty varieties that have been created in many years. Not only is it more compact than the older version of 'Monet,' it is also a sturdier cultivar. It is a unique variety that has unusual peach-colored bracts that are covered liberally with pink spots. The pink spots flow into pink bract margins. It blooms in mid-season and has dark green leaves.

- 'Hollystar Red' is a variety that is characterized by its red cythia in the center. The distinctive dark-red bracts stand upright, though they are slightly contorted. The dark green leaves have an unusual grayish-green center streak. The late season bloomer is a more compact cultivar.

- 'Saturnus Marble' is a companion to 'Saturnus Red' that blooms towards the late part of the mid-season. It is characterized by by creamy white-colored bracts, each of which has a light pink streak that extends the length of the center of the bract.

- 'Saturnus Twist' is characterized by somewhat twisted bracts that give the cultivar its name. Red bracts vary in the extent to which they are contorted. It has smaller, more twisted leaves than those on 'Saturnus Red.' It is a variety that flowers late in the mid-season.

Poinsettia Diseases and Their Causes

Poinsettia plants are susceptible to bacterial, fungal and viral diseases. Commercial growers grow poinsettias during the fall because of the cooler temperatures and shorter days. This practice ensures that plants that are available for sale just before or around Christmastime are at the peak of their attractiveness. Ironically, the necessary growing conditions for propagation can also create an environment that promotes the growth and development of diseases.

When diseases occur during the later phase of the growing process, plants may not be getting proper care, i.e., too much water, water that splashes on bracts and/or leaves, sitting in water (from decorative sleeves that retailers place them in,) or lack of space between plants, which prevents plants from getting adequate air circulation. Plants may not be getting cool enough temperatures that are essential for the final stage of growth prior to blooming. Some diseases, however, affect poinsettias at any state of growth.

Not all organisms are bad for poinsettias, as is evident from the economic benefit of the phytoplasma organism when poinsettias are growing in commercial production greenhouses. It seems ironic that a disease that might have a horribly adverse impact on other plants should have such a beneficial one on poinsettias that plants that aren't affected by the disease are less attractive, and therefore less appealing to consumers.

Fungal Diseases

Pythium Root Rot

Pythium root rot affects roots beneath the soil. Early symptoms include decaying or discolored feeder roots. Eventually, the cortex or root outer layer falls off. The exposed vascular tissue provides the entry point through which disease can spread up the entire plant stem, creating brown cankers. Mature plants may turn yellow and wilt because of lost root function. Rooted cuttings may develop brown, decaying roots. The upper part of the plant may not grow properly as the plant parts turn yellow. Plants that grow under extremely stressful situations may die. Plants whose root systems suffer from over exposure to soluble salts and water stress from excessive moisture are susceptible to several Pythium species. The fungal organisms spread when soil is infected, temperatures are too warm (between 50 to 86 degrees F,) or when plants come into contact with splashing or contaminated water.

Black Root Rot

Healthy plant roots are white. With black root rot, the disease begins at the tip of the roots when lesions or black bands develop. The diseased areas will look significantly different than healthy roots. As the disease spreads, the entire root system of infected plants turn black. When plant roots no longer function, plants don't get adequate nourishment. This leads to stunted plant growth, and eventually, wilting. Leaves may fall off after turning yellow.

The *Thielaviopsis* fungus causes black root rot disease. Other greenhouse plants may also develop the disease which is common among holly, pansy and petunia, all plants that are especially susceptible when grown in greenhouses. The main contributory factors in disease development are high soil pH and overly cool temperatures. Fungal diseases tend to thrive in excessively moist environments, too. Poinsettia plants are most likely to develop black root rot late in the growing cycle.

Rhizoctonia Root and Stem Rot

Signs and Symptoms

Young plants may be infected at the lower stem or roots. Brown, dry, and shrunken lesions may form at the base of stems. Depending on the extent of the infection, individual brown lesions may appear on roots, or they may turn entirely brown. Tops of plants may lose their leaves, or leaves may yellow. Stunted plant growth and wilting may also occur. As the infection progresses, the plant and nearby growing media may be covered by a brown mat of fungus.

Cause and Progression of the Disease

Rhizoctonia solani is a soil-borne fungus that spreads to other plants through contaminated surfaces, pots, tools, and when infected soil comes in contact with these things. Other conditions that encourage disease development are stem injury that occurs during planting, or when plants or rooted cuttings are planted too deep in the soil. Plants that are injured by soluble salts are more prone to infection.

Scab

At the onset of the disease, leaves develop small, round, blister-like spots. As the tan-to-brown spots expand, blotches of dead tissue form. Leaves turn yellow and fall off. Stems also develop lesions that are eventually covered with velvety-brown layer of fungus. Poinsettia scab is also called spot *anthracnose.* The *sphaceloma poinsettiae* fungus causes the disease, one that thrives in high humidity environments where there is too much soil moisture. Splashing water spreads the fungus to other plants.

Bortrytis Blight

Leaves develop spot lesions. Brownish-gray or tan blotches appear on bracts. Mature plants are most affected. A fuzzy gray layer of fungal spores and mycelium may cover affected areas. A symptom that explains why the disease is frequently called "gray mold." Plants and cuttings may be affected by stem blight, a condition that typically occurs on the crotches of branches. Stem cankers will cause leaves to fall off plants as distal parts of plants die.

Poinsettias are susceptible to *Bortrytis cinera* during all growth phases, especially when they are growing in commercial production greenhouses. It is such a common disease that most greenhouse-grown crops and plants may be affected by it. The fungus develops colonies on aging and dead plant tissues. Once fungal colonies are established, they produce large amounts of fungal spores that spread quickly – either through the air, or from splashing water. Spores also spread when people unknowingly handle diseased plants and then touch healthy plants. Over crowding and lack of adequate air flow, inadequate light (i.e., prolonged cloudy conditions,) and excessive moisture are all factors that encourage disease growth.

Powdery Mildew

Powdery mildew is a disease whose tell-tale signs are areas of white fungus and spores that appear on diseased bracts and leaves. Plant leaves may also be covered with brown and/or yellow spots. Although the disease doesn't kill plants, it renders plants unsaleable in commercial production. For houseplant owners, the plants are no longer attractive.

Oidium sp is the fungus that causes powdery mildew, the white fungus that grows on diseased plant tissues. Air and splashing water are two common ways by which the disease spreads. The powdery fungus is first evident on crowded plants that don't get sufficient light. Although the disease thrives in environments with humidity and moderate temperatures. It will develop and spread even in the absence of wetness on bracts and leaves.

Diseases Caused by Bacteria

Bacterial Soft Rot

Bacterial soft rot typically begins at stem bases, and as the disease progresses, it moves up the stem to the rest of the plant. When cuttings are affected, stems become mushy and soft. In older plants, stems will decay. Several species of the *Erwinia* bacteria cause the disease. Soft succulent cuttings are more prone to the disease. Growing environments with high humidity levels and temperatures create an ideal conditions for the development and spread of the disease. Other ways by which the disease spreads include diseased plant debris, growing media, soil, contaminated tools, or via splashing water. Insects can also carry the disease.

Bacterial Canker

Diseased plant stems develop long, brown streaks from water-soaking. Water logging spots also occur on leaves. Stems develop large lesions that turn into cankers before cracking. With progression of the disease, leaves fall off the canker-covered stems, and plants ultimately die. *Corynebacterium flaccumfaciens* is the bacteria that causes bacterial canker. Poinsettias are most susceptible in the later growing phase. When the growing environment is too warm or moist, conditions are ripe for disease to occur. The disease spreads via contaminated tools, when hands touch diseased plants before handling healthy plants, or when splashing water allows the bacteria to travel.

Viral and Phytoplasma Diseases

Poinsettia Mosaic Virus

Infected leaves may be covered with a scattering of yellow spots. Dead tissue may appear in the center of some angular-shaped spots. Mosaic mottle can also occur because of the virus. PnMV (Poinsettia Mosaic Virus,) like other plant-specific types of mosaic virus is primarily spread when contaminated hands or tools touch healthy plants. Plants are more susceptible to the disease when grown in cool conditions - a temperature range of between 61 and 68 degrees F.

Poinsettia Branch-Inducing Phytoplasma

Ironically, some of the most admired characteristics of poinsettia plants, including free, multi-flowering branches and compact growing form, are not the result of plant genetics. These desirable traits are caused by systematic phytoplasma infection. PoiBI is related to organisms belonging to the peach X-disease group. This phytoplasma is the first disease to have beneficial production traits. When researchers removed the disease agent from plants, they were no longer compact and bushy. Strangely, because the disease-free plants produce fewer flowers, grow taller and more spindly, the fact that they lack the branching trait that makes them bushier and produce more flowers makes them less profitable for growers and less popular with consumers.

Managing Diseases

The best way to control poinsettia diseases is by preventing them from developing in the first place. Doing that involves a comprehensive approach that requires th at plants get the proper care, and that the growing area is always clean. Good sanitation practices include always using sterile soil, and cleaning and disinfecting growing surfaces and tools. The fungi, bacteria and other disease-causing organisms will survive in organic matter such as dead plant debris, soil and water - especially if the growing area isn't thoroughly sanitized.

Make sure your sanitation practices are thorough enough, use the following safe sanitation guidelines as a checklist.

- Never allow diseased plants and their debris or soil to stay in the same area where healthy plants grow.

- Make sure your growing area is always clean. Use disinfectants or germicides to sanitize it.

- When propagating plants from cuttings, always use a sterilized growing medium. When transplanting cuttings, follow the same practices. Make sure you sterilize your tools before taking cuttings or transplanting or planting plants.

- Make sure you don't allow organic material such as fallen leaves or bracts to remain in the growing area.

- If you see unhealthy-looking leaves, remove them promptly.

- When watering plants, don't allow the watering can to come into contact with soil. Water plants in such a way that water doesn't splash on leaves or bracts, or from plant to plant.

Safe Plant Care Practices

The way you care for your poinsettias can also be helpful in preventing diseases from developing in the first place.

- Take care when handling plants and or cuttings – including during propagation or transplantation.

- Make sure that you keep plants far enough apart – even those that are not planted together.

- Ensure there is sufficient ventilation in growing areas so you can keep humidity levels down.

Propagating Poinsettias

The best way to propagate poinsettias is by taking a cutting. Before taking the cutting, be sure that your instrument – be in a pruning shears or knife, is properly sterilized. Take cuttings from new growth for the year, not from the previous year's growth. Make a cut below a leaf node, making sure that the length of your cutting is about three or four inches long. Also make sure that you aren't trying to take a cutting from a patent-protected variety because it is illegal for anyone other than the patent holder to propagate cuttings from protected plants. Remove the lower leaves from the stem.

Since poinsettias don't do well where there is too much water, these cuttings should be rooted right in a growing media. You may want to dip your cutting into a rooting hormone to help expedite the rooting process. Another advantage to doing this is that rooting hormones also contain a fungicide. All of your supplies should be sterile, including tools, pots and growing medium. You can root cuttings in plant trays or peat pots that you can then transplant when cuttings are four inches taller than they were when you started rooting them.

Wait until your cuttings have leaves before transplanting them. If you intend to root several cuttings simultaneously, place them far enough apart that each cutting will get sufficient air circulation. Moisten the growing medium, but don't saturate it. Allow it to dry out before you water it again to prevent excessive moisture from promoting disease growth.

Although most commercial growers resort to liquid chemical fungicides to combat fungal diseases in production greenhouses, this is probably not a wise course of action in the home, or in any environment where small children, animals, and people with chronic health conditions are present. An effective alternative to harsh chemicals is the use of organic products whose main active ingredient is pure neem oil. Neem oil coats leaves and other plant surfaces, repelling insects in the process and prevents fungal spores from spreading. it's also effective as a leaf cleaner. You can find neem oil in several Garden Safe products. Most home improvement stores and garden center stores sell these products and other organic neem oil-based fungicides as well.

Holiday plants are easily found and reasonably priced. They are widely available in grocery stores, in garden centers, at florists and at discount store chains. Amaryllis and Paperwhites are often sold in boxed kits that are the perfect gift for co-workers, to use as host or hostess gifts, or to give to yourself. No matter where you live, the addition of live holiday plants will transform your holiday decorating. Once you discover how fun and easy it is to take care of and reforce bulbs or get plants to rebloom, you may decide to add the festive fun of these plants to your holiday decorating and gift giving traditions.

Chapter 4: Additional Resources

Suppliers

There are many suppliers of amaryllis, paperwhites and poinsettias available. For buying actual bulbs in the US, the following suppliers are reliable and have a good selection:

Amaryllis Bulb Company (http://www.amaryllis.com/) – This company has been in business for several years and is based in Florida. They carry large flowering amaryllis, double amaryllis as well as dwarf, rare and African varieties. Ordering can be done online or through their catalog.

White Flower Farm (http://www.whiteflowerfarm.com) – In business since 1950, they carry amaryllis and paperwhites as well as a wide variety of other plants and bulbs. They're based in Connecticut and offer online ordering.

If you are in the UK, Spalding Plant and Bulb Co (http://www.spaldingbulb.co.uk) offers about a dozen or so varieties of amaryllis, plus paperwhites and one variety of poinsettia. They have been in the mail order business for over 65 years and provide excellent customer service.

For Poinsettias, since these are fully grown plants delivered with the expectation of a limited lifespan, finding a reliable local grower or supplier is your best option.

Additional Research and Sources of Care for Amaryllis

Being widely grown by home gardeners, there is quite a bit of information available for the amaryllis. Here are a few sites that offer more reading for your continued education:

University of Florida – IFAS Extension (http://edis.ifas.ufl.edu/topic_amaryllis) – Amaryllis cultivation information

Understanding and Producing Amaryllis
(http://www.clemson.edu/psapublishing/pages/HORT/HORTLF63.PDF) – Clemson Extension's cultivation and propagation publication in PDF format

<u>University of California Cooperative Extension</u>
(http://ucanr.org/sites/UrbanHort/files/80184.pdf) – Another PDF publication with helpful information on care and propagation

Additional Research and Sources of Care for Paperwhites

<u>Pickling Your Paperwhites</u>
(http://www.hort.cornell.edu/miller/bulb/Pickling_your_Paperwhites.pdf) – a PDF publication by Cornell Professor of Horticulture, William B. Miller on using alcohol to limit the growth of paperwhite narcissus

<u>Miami–Dade County Extension</u> (http://miami-dade.ifas.ufl.edu/old/programs/commorn/publications/paperwhite-narcissus-production.PDF) – an overview on care, forcing and pests in PDF format

Additional Research and Sources of Care for Poinsettias

<u>Iowa State University Extension</u>
(http://www.extension.iastate.edu/Publications/RG316.pdfhttp://www.extension.iastate.edu/Publications/RG316.pdf) – An overview on poinsettia care in PDF

<u>Purdue University Cooperative Extension Service</u> (http://www.hort.purdue.edu/ext/HO-073.pdf) – another overview on poinsettia care, but with helpful diagrams on cutting back your plants in the autumn.

CPSIA information can be obtained
at www.ICGtesting.com
Printed in the USA
LVHW071348260419
615674LV00009B/139/P